The Atlas of the Seven Continents™

EUROPE
Wendy Vierow

The Rosen Publishing Group's
PowerKids Press™
New York

For Chris, who loves atlases

Published in 2004 by The Rosen Publishing Group, Inc.
29 East 21st Street, New York, NY 10010

First Edition

Editor: Frances E. Ruffin
Book Design: Maria E. Melendez
Layout Design: Eric DePalo

Photo Credits: Cover and title page, map of Europe, world map © Visible Earth/NASA; p. 5 (bottom) world illustrations by Maria Melendez; p. 7 © 2001 Todd Marshall; pp. 9, 11, 13, 17 (Europe map) © GeoAtlas; p. 15 map illustrated by Eric DePalo; p. 17 (Iberian Lynxes) © Reuters NewMedia Inc./CORBIS; p. 17 (white stork) © Chris Hellier/CORBIS; p. 17 (Alpine Ibexes) © Maurizio Lanini/CORBIS; p. 17 (bear) © Digital Vision; p. 19 (Grape harvest) © Vince Streano/CORBIS; p. 19 (unloading fish) © Michael S. Yamashita/CORBIS; p. 19 (businesspeople) © Royalty-Free/CORBIS; p. 21 (Bagpipe player) © David Ball/CORBIS; p. 21 (Polish boy) © Peter Turnley/CORBIS; p. 21 (girls in Andalucian Dress) © Anders Ryman/CORBIS.

Vierow, Wendy.
Europe / Wendy Vierow.
    p. cm. — (The atlas of the seven continents)
Includes index.
ISBN 0-8239-6691-7 (library binding)
1. Europe—Geography—Juvenile literature. 2. Europe—Description and travel—Juvenile literature. 3. Natural history—Europe—Juvenile literature. I. Title.
D900 .V54 2004
914—dc21

2002154688

Manufactured in the United States of America

CPSIA Compliance Information: Batch #CR017250PK: For Further Information Contact Rosen Publishing, New York, New York at 1-800-237-9932

Contents

Earth's Continents and Oceans

Europe is Earth's smallest continent after Australia. A continent is a large body of land. Earth's seven continents are Africa, Antarctica, Asia, Australia, Europe, North America, and South America. Earth's continents are surrounded by the Arctic, Atlantic, Indian, and Pacific Oceans. Some **geographers** call the southern parts of the Atlantic, Indian, and Pacific Oceans the Antarctic Ocean or the Southern Ocean. Scientists think that, more than 200 million years ago, there was one giant continent called Pangaea, which was surrounded by one huge ocean called Panthalassa. Over time Pangaea broke into smaller continents. Scientists believe that the continents are still moving. Continents move because Earth's plates, or large sheets of rock, float on partly melted rock from deep inside Earth. When plates move, they change Earth's surface. Movements of Earth's plates cause many **earthquakes** in Europe's Mediterranean region. They also cause volcanoes to form and to erupt, or to have hot, melted rock pour out from deep inside Earth to Earth's surface. Active volcanoes in Europe include Italy's Stromboli, Mount Etna, and Mount Vesuvius.

Arctic Ocean

Europe

Asia

North America

Atlantic Ocean

Africa

Indian Ocean

Australia

South America

Pacific Ocean

Antarctica

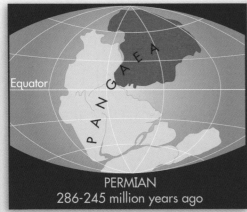

PERMIAN
286-245 million years ago

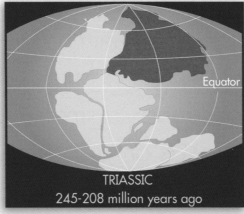

TRIASSIC
245-208 million years ago

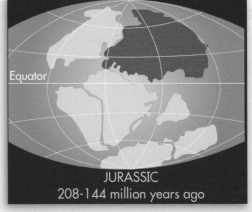

JURASSIC
208-144 million years ago

Above: *This is a photograph of Earth taken from space. The small maps show how the continent of Pangaea may have broken up. Some scientists say that, because Europe and Asia (in red) are not separated by water, they are one continent.*

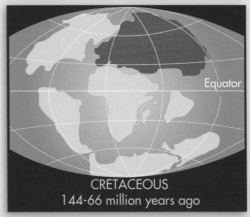

CRETACEOUS
144-66 million years ago

NORTH AMERICA

EUROPE

ASIA

AFRICA

Equator

SOUTH AMERICA

AUSTRALIA

ANTARCTICA

PRESENT DAY
From 66 million years ago

The Mesozoic **era**, which lasted from about 245 million to 66 million years ago, is also called the Age of Dinosaurs. Scientists study fossils, the hardened remains from dead animals, from that time to find out about dinosaurs and other life during the Mesozoic era.

During Europe's Mesozoic era, a kind of shark called a *Hybodus*, which grew up to 8 feet (2.5 m) long, hunted for fish and reptiles in the water. A **reptile** called a *Bernissartia*, which looked like a small crocodile, ate fish and other small animals. In the air was a flying reptile called an *Anurognathus*. It measured 20 inches (51 cm) from wing to wing. On the ground was a small, meat-eating mammal called a *Morganucodon*. It was only 4 inches (10 cm) long. The *Baryonyx*, a dinosaur that was 36 feet (11 m) long, ate a lot of fish to keep its weight around 4 tons (3.5 t)! Another dinosaur, called a *Dacentrurus*, was about 15 feet (4.5 m) long, had spikes on its back, and ate plants. Plants of the Mesozoic era included gingko trees and conifers, or trees with cones. There were also cycads, or trees that looked like palms or ferns, and the first flowering plants.

Fossils of an Eotyrannus were found off the southern coast of England, on the Isle of Wight. The name Eotyrannus *means "early tyrant." "Tyrant" means "cruel ruler,"* and these meat-eating animals were among the dinosaurs who ruled the world about 120 to 125 million years ago. They were smaller, early relatives of the Tyrannosaurus rex, *a dinosaur found in North America.* Eotyrannus *were 15 feet (4.5 m) long. Like their cousin* Tyrannosaurus rex, *they had a mouthful of sharp teeth, but much longer claws.*

How to Read a Map

You can find different maps in an atlas. Special features on maps make them easier to read. A map's title tells what the map shows. Often the title can be found in the map key or legend. The map key or legend tells what the **symbols** on a map mean.

The map scale shows how the size of a map compares to the actual size of a place on Earth. A compass rose or north pointer shows directions on a map. Earth's four main directions are north, south, east, and west. **Latitude** and **longitude** lines also show directions. Latitude lines run from east to west. Longitude lines run from north to south. The **equator** is 0° latitude. The **prime meridian** is 0° longitude. The prime meridian, or Greenwich Meridian, passes through Greenwich, England, in Europe. The world's 24 time zones start at the prime meridian. Each time zone is 15° wide. For every time zone east of the prime meridian, one hour is added. For every time zone west of the prime meridian, one hour is subtracted. For example, when it is 12:00 P.M. in the city of Greenwich, England, it is 7:00 A.M. in New York City, five hours' difference.

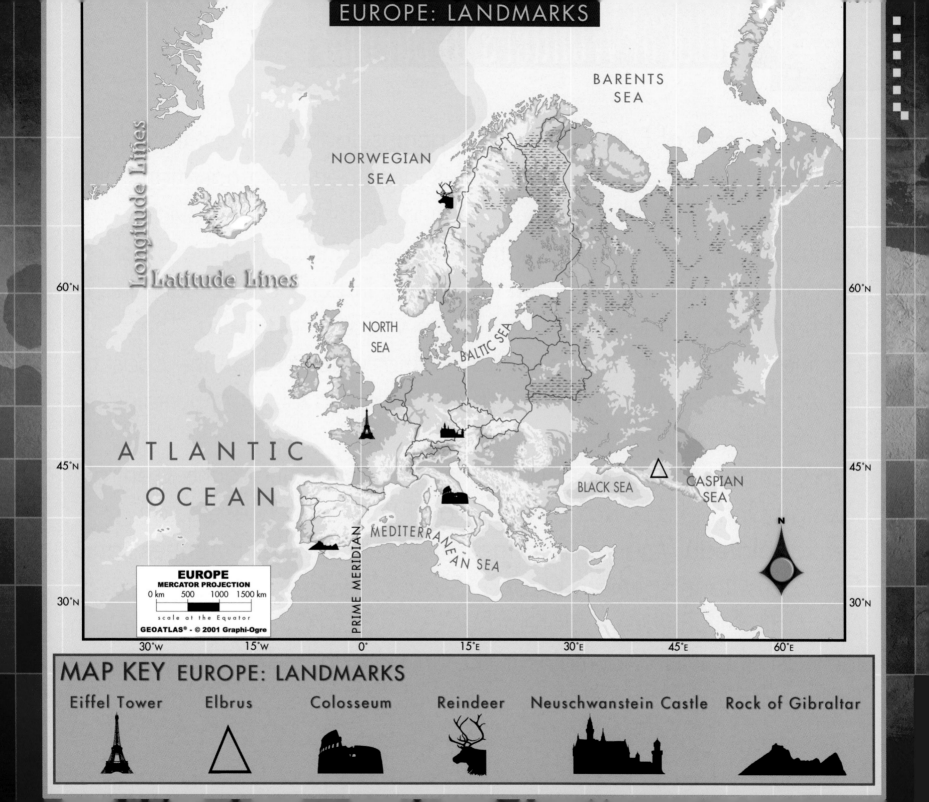

EUROPE: LANDMARKS

BARENTS
SEA

NORWEGIAN
SEA

Longitude Lines

Latitude Lines

60°N

NORTH
SEA

BALTIC SEA

ATLANTIC

OCEAN

45°N

BLACK SEA

CASPIAN
SEA

MEDITERRANEAN SEA

PRIME MERIDIAN

EUROPE
MERCATOR PROJECTION
0 km   500   1000 1500 km
scale at the Equator
GEOATLAS® - © 2001 Graphi-Ogre

30°N

30°W   15°W   0°   15°E   30°E   45°E   60°E

N

60°N

45°N

30°N

MAP KEY EUROPE: LANDMARKS

Eiffel Tower   Elbrus   Colosseum   Reindeer   Neuschwanstein Castle   Rock of Gibraltar

Natural Wonders of Europe

The continent of Europe is a large **peninsula** that juts out from the continent of Asia. The coastline of this large peninsula has many other peninsulas, such as the Balkan Peninsula and the Scandinavian Peninsula. Many islands off **mainland** Europe, including the British Isles and Iceland, are also part of Europe. In Europe's far north lies a cold, dry place where trees cannot grow, called a **tundra**. The continent's Northern European Plain, which extends from the coast of the Atlantic Ocean in France eastward to Russia's Ural Mountains, has excellent soil for farming.

In Central Europe, there is higher land that includes the Central Russian Upland, as well as Spain and Portugal's Meseta, or central **plateau**. Mountain ranges such as the Alps, Pyrenees, and Caucasus lie in southern Europe. Mount Elbrus, in the Caucasus Mountains, is Europe's highest peak at 18,510 feet (5,642 m). In the east, the Ural Mountains make up part of the boundary between Europe and Asia.

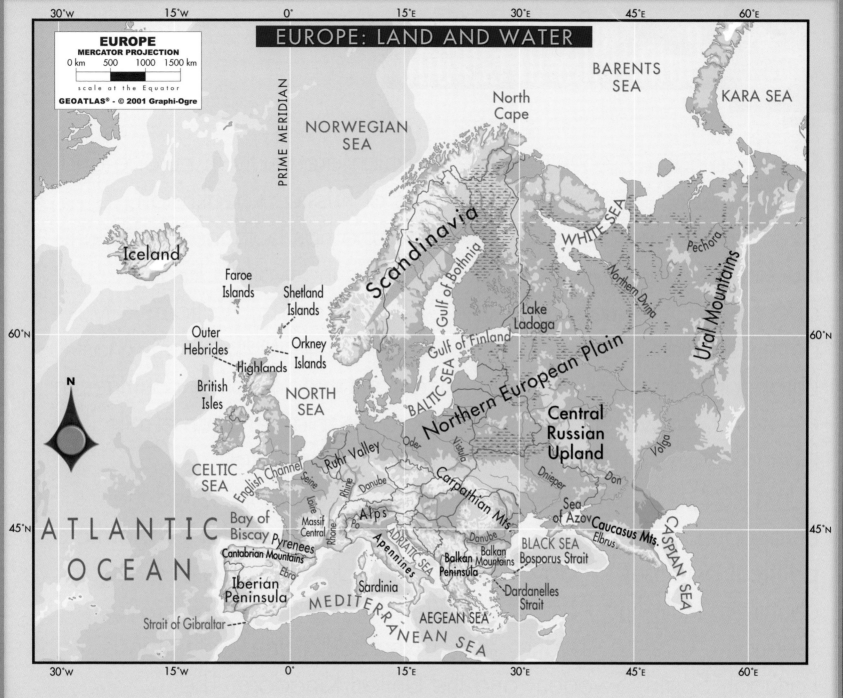

EUROPE: LAND AND WATER

EUROPE
MERCATOR PROJECTION

0 km   500   1000 1500 km

scale at the Equator

GEOATLAS® - © 2001 Graphi-Ogre

BARENTS SEA

KARA SEA

NORWEGIAN SEA

North Cape

WHITE SEA

Pechora

PRIME MERIDIAN

Iceland

Scandinavia

Gulf of Bothnia

Lake Ladoga

Northern Dvina

Ural Mountains

Faroe Islands

Shetland Islands

Outer Hebrides

Orkney Islands

Highlands

60°N

British Isles

NORTH SEA

Gulf of Finland

BALTIC SEA

Northern European Plain

Central Russian Upland

Volga

N

CELTIC SEA

English Channel

Seine

Ruhr Valley

Oder

Vistula

Dnieper

Don

Loire

Rhine

Danube

Carpathian Mts.

Sea of Azov

Bay of Biscay

Massif Central

Alps

Rhone

Po

Caucasus Mts.

CASPIAN SEA

45°N

Pyrenees

ADRIATIC SEA

Danube

BLACK SEA

Elbrus

Cantabrian Mountains

Apennines

Balkan Mountains

Bosporus Strait

ATLANTIC OCEAN

Ebro

Balkan Peninsula

Iberian Peninsula

Sardinia

Dardanelles Strait

Strait of Gibraltar

MEDITERRANEAN SEA

AEGEAN SEA

Bays, gulfs, and seas lie between Europe's many peninsulas. The Caspian Sea, which lies in both Europe and Asia, is the world's largest lake at 143,550 square miles (371,793 sq km). The northern shore of the Caspian Sea is Europe's lowest point, 92 feet (28 m) below sea level. Pouring into the Caspian Sea is Europe's longest river, the Volga, which flows 2,194 miles (3,531 km) through Russia.

Countries of Europe

Europe has 47 countries, five of which are partly in Europe and partly in Asia. These are the countries of Russia, Kazakhstan, Azerbaijan, Georgia, and Turkey. Europe has both the largest and the smallest country in the world. Russia is the world's largest country at 6,592,850 square miles (17,075,400 sq km). Vatican City is Earth's smallest country at about ⅙ square mile (0.4 sq km). Most European countries are small in size compared to other countries in the world. However, Europe has more people per square mile (km) than does any other continent on Earth, except Asia.

In 1993, 12 European countries formed a group called the European Union. The members of this group joined for **economic** and **political** purposes. Today, the European Union is made of 15 countries, including Austria, Belgium, Denmark, Finland, France, Germany, Greece, Ireland, Italy, Luxembourg, the Netherlands, Portugal, Spain, Sweden, and the United Kingdom. The headquarters of the European Union is in Brussels, Belgium.

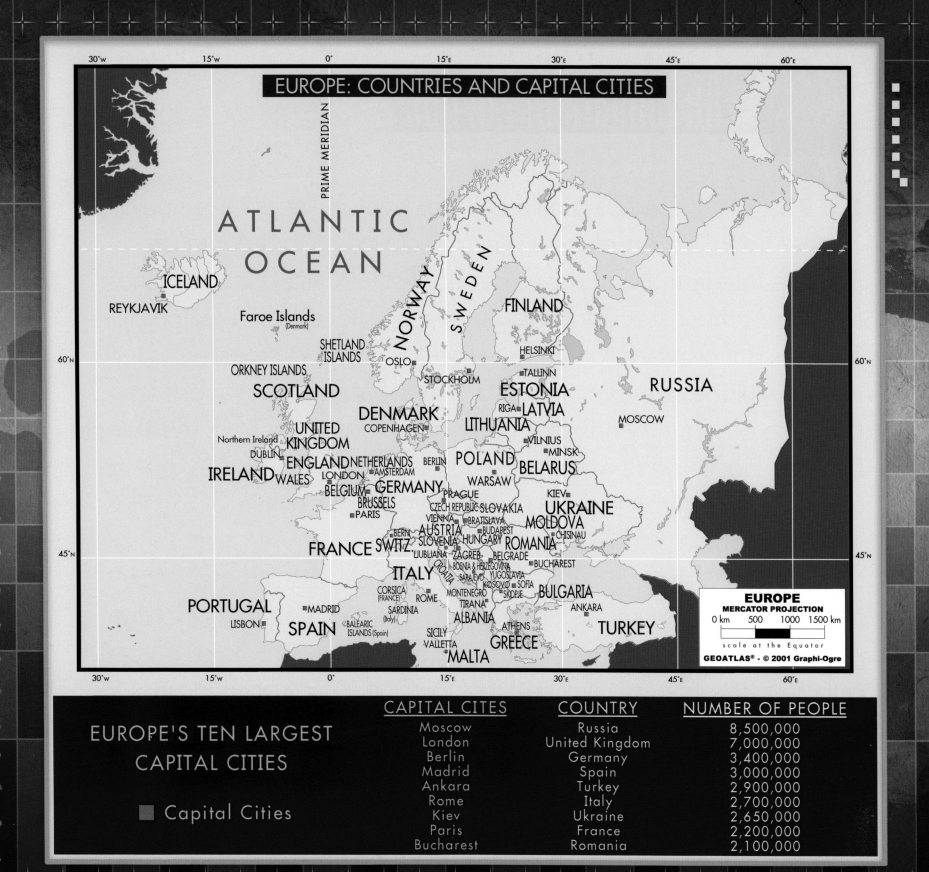

EUROPE: COUNTRIES AND CAPITAL CITIES

PRIME MERIDIAN

ATLANTIC OCEAN

ICELAND
REYKJAVIK

Faroe Islands
(Denmark)

SHETLAND ISLANDS

ORKNEY ISLANDS

SCOTLAND

NORWAY

SWEDEN

FINLAND
HELSINKI

OSLO
STOCKHOLM
TALLINN
ESTONIA
RIGA LATVIA
LITHUANIA

RUSSIA
MOSCOW

DENMARK
COPENHAGEN

VILNIUS
MINSK

Northern Ireland

UNITED KINGDOM

DUBLIN

ENGLAND NETHERLANDS
AMSTERDAM

BERLIN
POLAND
WARSAW

BELARUS

KIEV

IRELAND WALES

BELGIUM GERMANY
PRAGUE
CZECH REPUBLIC SLOVAKIA

UKRAINE

LONDON

BRUSSELS
PARIS

VIENNA
BRATISLAVA
BUDAPEST

MOLDOVA
CHISINAU

BERN AUSTRIA
SLOVENIA HUNGARY
LJUBLJANA ZAGREB

ROMANIA
BELGRADE
BUCHAREST

FRANCE SWITZ

ITALY

CROATIA
BOSNIA & HERZEGOVINA
SARAJEVO YUGOSLAVIA
KOSOVO SOFIA
MONTENEGRO SKOPJE

BULGARIA

CORSICA (FRANCE)
ROME
TIRANA

ANKARA

PORTUGAL

MADRID
SARDINIA (Italy)

ALBANIA

ATHENS

TURKEY

LISBON
SPAIN

BALEARIC ISLANDS (Spain)

SICILY
VALLETTA
MALTA

GREECE

EUROPE
MERCATOR PROJECTION

0 km   500   1000 1500 km

scale at the Equator

GEOATLAS® - © 2001 Graphi-Ogre

EUROPE'S TEN LARGEST CAPITAL CITIES

■ Capital Cities

CAPITAL CITES	COUNTRY	NUMBER OF PEOPLE
Moscow	Russia	8,500,000
London	United Kingdom	7,000,000
Berlin	Germany	3,400,000
Madrid	Spain	3,000,000
Ankara	Turkey	2,900,000
Rome	Italy	2,700,000
Kiev	Ukraine	2,650,000
Paris	France	2,200,000
Bucharest	Romania	2,100,000

The Climate of Europe

Most of Europe has a mild climate. Climate includes temperature, or how hot or cold a place is, and precipitation, or how much moisture falls from the sky. Europe receives about 20 to 60 inches (51–152 cm) of precipitation every year. Europe's mild temperature and amount of precipitation are good for growing crops.

Many things can affect climate. Europe's climate is mostly mild because of warm winds that blow across the land from the Atlantic Ocean. Places near water are often warmer than places that are away from water. Many places in Europe are within 300 miles (483 km) of the Atlantic Ocean.

Elevation, or how high a place is, also affects climate. Most places at high elevations have a cool, wet climate. Most of the Alps, Europe's largest mountain range, have this climate. Europe's climate also remains mild because Europe's mountains do not form a large enough barrier, or wall, to block the warm ocean winds from reaching the rest of the continent. Latitude and moisture affect climate, and places closest to the equator are warm and wet.

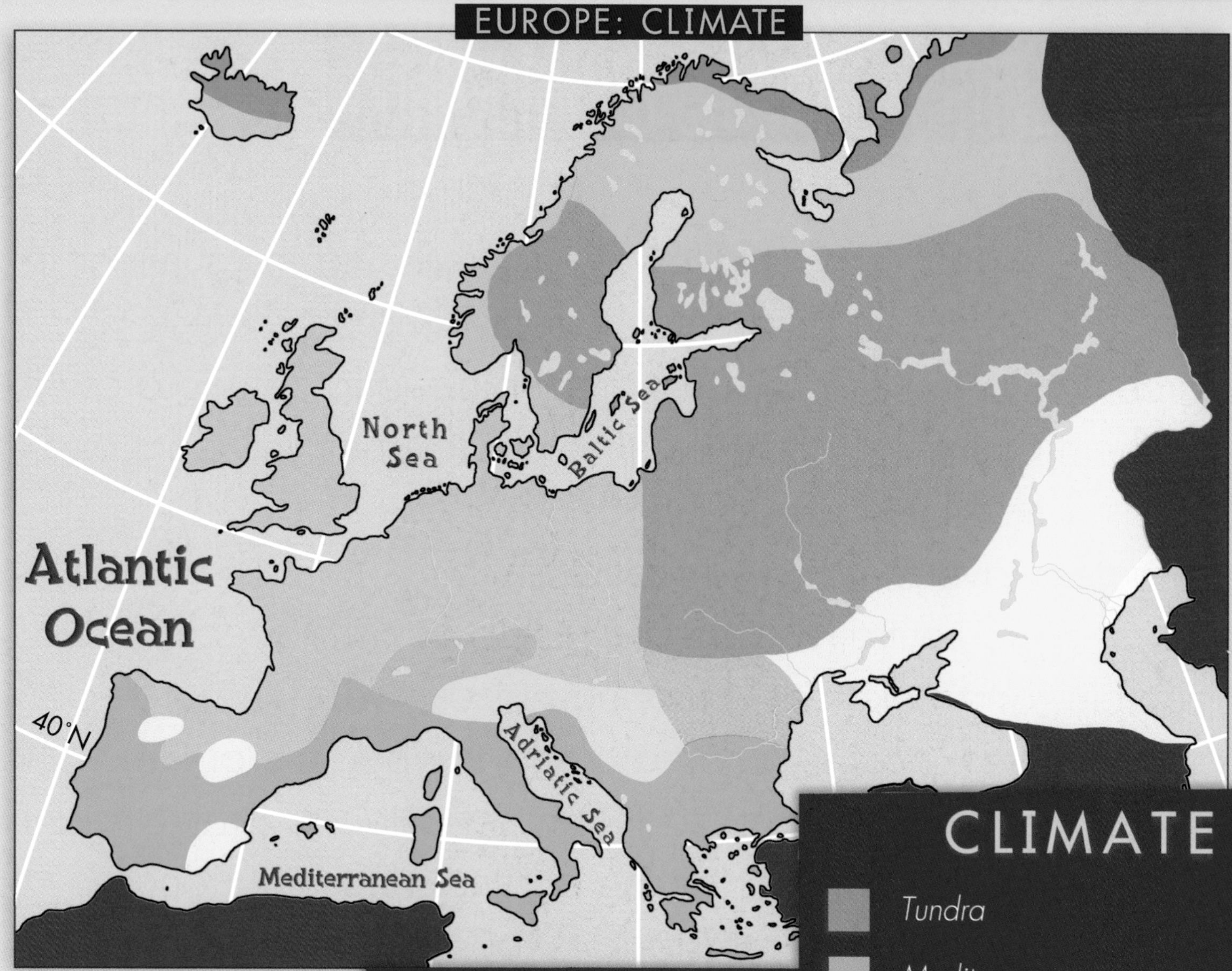

North
Sea

Baltic Sea

Atlantic
Ocean

40°N

Adriatic Sea

Mediterranean Sea

Countries in southern Europe, including Greece, Italy, Portugal, and Spain, have short, mild winters and warm summers. Parts of countries in northern Europe that have arctic tundras, such as Norway, Sweden, Finland, and Russia, are among the coldest places in Europe.

CLIMATE

Warm Summer

Cool Summer

Subarctic

Marine West Coast

Tundra

Mediterranean

Humid Subtropical

Semiarid

Arid

Highlands

Europe's Plants and Animals

Mosses, shrubs, and wildflowers grow during the summer in the northern tundra and high mountains of Europe. Forests of evergreens and fir trees such as larch, pine, and spruce grow in the northern countries. In the North live large brown bears and tiny lemmings, animals related to the mouse. Eagles, falcons, nightingales, ravens, and many different birds fly in central Europe. Also in central Europe are forests of ash, beech, birch, elm, maple, and oak trees. European bison live in the protected Belovezha Forest. This is an area along the borders of the countries of Belarus and Poland that is set aside to protect plants and animals. It contains part of the original forest that once covered a great part of **prehistoric** Europe. Olive trees and cork oak trees grow to the south, along the Mediterranean coast. Barbary apes, the only wild monkeys in Europe, live on the Rock of Gibraltar, near southern Spain. Fish such as anchovy, cod, salmon, sardine, trout, and tuna swim in the Atlantic Ocean and many of Europe's seas.

These Iberian lynx kittens are in a Spanish zoo. Today very few lynx live in the wild.

This is a European brown bear. Brown bears are Europe's largest meat-eating animals.

White storks often build their nests on rooftops of houses in northern European cities.

Alpine ibex are wild goats that live in the Alps. They were photographed in Italy's Gran Paradiso National Park.

Making a Living in Europe

Although most countries in Europe have few natural **resources**, such as oil and trees for lumber, Europe has many skilled workers to help its economy grow. Workers in Europe manufacture more goods than do workers on any other continent. Products manufactured in Europe include automobiles, chemicals, machinery, and cloth. Russia produces large amounts of iron ore and is one of the leading mining countries in the world. Europe mines about one-third of the world's coal in such countries as Russia, Germany, and Poland. Europe also mines about one-third of the world's natural gas. Most Europeans work in service jobs in fields such as education, transportation, and finance, which includes banking. Farms take up about one-half of Europe's land. Europe leads the world in the production of barley, oats, potatoes, rye, sugar beets, and wheat. Countries along the Mediterranean coast, such as Italy and Greece, grow most of the world's olives. Norway and Russia, which have many miles (km) of coastline along Europe's seas, lead the continent in fishing.

Tuscany

ITALY

Mediterranean Sea

Workers at a vineyard in Tuscany, Italy, pour out buckets of grapes that will be made into red wine.

Barents Sea

RUSSIA

The Russian fishermen shown here are unloading fish into wooden crates to be sold at a fish market.

Prague

CZECH REPUBLIC

These businesspeople work in Prague, a city in the Czech Republic.

The People of Europe

The first great civilization in Europe reached its height about 2,500 years ago in Greece. During the Roman **Empire**, which reached its height about 2000 years ago, **Christianity** was brought to Europe from Asia and became the empire's official religion. Today most Europeans practice Christianity. Some Europeans practice **Judaism** or **Islam**. Many European languages, such as Italian, French, and Spanish, are based on Latin, a language spoken by ancient Romans. During the Roman Empire, the Celts lived in what is now Ireland, Scotland, Wales, and parts of England and France. The Celts spoke Celtic languages such as Irish, Welsh, and Scottish Gaelic. From the late 700s to about 1100, the Vikings of Scandinavia sailed to Iceland, Greenland, and North America. They spoke Germanic languages and were great sailors. Slavs, who lived mostly in eastern Europe and spoke Slavic, or Slavonic, languages, created the Great Moravian Empire in Central Europe in the 800s. Today Europe still has many different **ethnic groups** that follow their own ways of life and speak their own languages.

The boy carrying the newspaper lives in Gdansk, Poland, which is in eastern Europe. He speaks Polish, a Slavic language.

The bagpiper is from Scotland, which is part of the United Kingdom. He is wearing a tartan, or a wool cloth with a special plaid pattern.

These two young girls are attending a spring fair in Seville, Spain. They are dressed in costumes worn by Spanish children many years ago.

A Scientist in Europe

One of Earth's most famous volcanoes is Mount Etna on the Italian island of Sicily. Mount Etna's first recorded eruption was about 2,700 years ago. Mount Etna has erupted more than 260 times since then. In 2002, earthquakes caused Mount Etna to erupt again. Sonia Calvari is a **volcanologist** who studies Mount Etna and other volcanoes. When Mount Etna erupted in 2001, Calvari and other scientists studied the volcano. Calvari noted that amphibole crystals were present in the lava, or melted rock, that flowed from Mount Etna. This kind of crystal can cause explosions. Some scientists fear that, in the future, Mount Etna's eruptions could be more explosive. One of Mount Etna's worst eruptions was in 1669, when 20,000 people died during its four-month-long eruption. While Calvari was at Mount Etna in 1989, a powerful wind began to push Calvari and the scientists toward the erupting volcano's deep and fiery crater. Even though her job has its scary moments, Calvari continues to study volcanoes. Her work helps others to understand volcanoes better.

Glossary

Christianity (kris-chee-A-nih-tee) A faith based on the teachings of Jesus Christ and the Bible.

earthquakes (URTH-kwayks) Shakings of Earth's crust because of the movement of large pieces of land, called plates, that run into each other.

economic (eh-kuh-NAH-mik) Having to do with the production and supply and demands for goods and services.

empire (EM-pyr) A large area controlled by one ruler.

equator (ih-KWAY-tur) An imaginary line around the middle of Earth.

era (ER-uh) A period of time or history.

ethnic groups (ETH-nik GROOPS) Groups of people having the same race, beliefs, practices, or language, or belonging to the same country.

geographers (jee-AH-gruh-ferz) Scientists who study features of Earth.

Islam (IS-lom) A faith based on the teachings of Mohammed and the Koran.

Judaism (JOO-dee-ih-zum) The faith followed by Jews, based on teachings in the Old Testament of the Bible.

latitude (LA-tih-tood) The distance north or south of the equator, measured by degrees.

longitude (LON-jih-tood) The distance east or west of the prime meridian, measured by degrees.

mainland (MAYN-land) A large area of land near an island.

peninsula (peh-NIN-suh-luh) An area of land surrounded by water on three sides.

plateau (pla-TOH) A broad, flat, high piece of land.

political (puh-LIH-tih-kul) Having to do with the work of government and public affairs.

prehistoric (pree-his-TOR-ik) The time before written history.

prime meridian (PRYM meh-RIH-dee-en) The imaginary line that passes through Greenwich, England, and that is 0° longitude.

reptile (REP-tyl) A cold-blooded animal with lungs and scales.

resources (REE-sors-ez) Supplies or sources of energy or useful materials.

symbols (SIM-bulz) Objects or pictures that stand for something else.

tundra (TUN-druh) A frozen area with no trees and with black soil.

volcanologist (vol-kuh-NAH-luh-jist) A person who studies volcanoes.

Index

A
amphibole crystals, 22

B
Balkan Peninsula, 10
Barbary apes, 16
Belovezha Forest, 16
British Isles, 10

C
Calvari, Sonia, 22
Celts, 20
Christianity, 20
climate, 14

D
dinosaurs, 6

E
earthquakes, 4, 22
Elbrus, Mount, 10
equator, 8, 14
Etna, Mount, 4, 22
European Union, 12

F
finance, 18
fossils, 6

I
Islam, 20

J
Judaism, 20

P
Pangaea, 4
Panthalassa, 4
prime meridian, 8

R
resources, 18
Roman Empire, 20
Russia, 12, 18

U
Ural Mountains, 10

V
Vatican City, 12
Vikings, 20
volcanoes, 4, 22

Web Sites

Due to the changing nature of Internet links, PowerKids Press has developed an online list of Web sites related to the subject of this book. This site is updated regularly. Please use this link to access the list:

www.powerkidslinks.com/asc/europe/